MADAM WONG'S GUIDE TO MEN AND OTHER DIFFICULTIES

By Eliza Bussey
Orange Blossom Publications

IN REMEMBRANCE OF HEZ JAMES BUSSEY
July 13, 1923 to March 13th, 1994

"Mark how fleeting and paltry is the estate of man - yesterday in embryo, tomorrow a mummy or ashes. So for the hairsbreadth of time assigned to thee, live rationally, and part with life cheerfully, as drops the ripe olive, extolling the season that bore it and the tree that matured it."

Marcus Aurelius   A.D. 121-180

This book is dedicated with great appreciation and love:

To Dr. Charles Duan Roth, my Master Teacher,
and Spiritual Midwife.

And to my parents,
Mary Ruth and Hez Bussey

May the light of goodness and love that you bestowed on me, travel out beyond the farthest stars of the galaxy, and be a song for Angels.

Acknowledgments:

Jo-Ann Power, my editorial sparring partner and confidant.
Patsy Welch, for her delightful illustration of Madam Wong.
Charles C. Colley for his artful and endearing illustrations.
Craig Hines for layout and design.

Special acknowledgments go to:
My sister, Susan Bussey, and my supportive and tolerant friends, Kerry Donahue Sweeney, Kathy Ray, Rhonda and Joe Ripperger, Martha Sandlin, Charlotte Kuenen, David Kirstein, Michael Messinger, David Perry and Denyce Graves.

FOREWORD

Ever since my late husband Wa Shin and I opened our first Chinese herbal store in fishing village near Ningbo, along the salt sea, young girls and their mothers would come to my shop for more than tofu and Jasmine tea. It seem they want to know more than how to cure wart on big toe or ease labor pain. It seem they want to know how Madam Wong would handle this or that problem. For years I would dry the eyes of love sick young girls, and take them back to my kitchen for secret herbal drink aimed at easing heartache, followed with a quiet hug, and some motherly advice. To be honest, the young butterfly whose wings were drooped in despair, would fly off with a smile on face, and renewed sense of herself. It made my heart sing with joy when my butterflies flew higher than the tallest trees in Quingdao Province.

Years later, Wa Shin and I moved to America, and opened our own herbal store in New York's China town. There, a new group of young women requested Madam Wong's special elixirs.

As time pass, the boundaries between East and West began to blur, as Madam Wong hear many Western stories and experience Western life.

She began to mix American stories with her Chinese tales. (She learn, the strongest elixir might contain one part Brer Rabbit, two parts Confucius, with a dash of Sigmund Freud.)

After years of repeating same stories over and over, I decided to put my home-grown wisdom to paper.

With deep love and appreciation, I dedicate the following meditations to my butterflies of Quingdao Province.

THOUGHTS OF THE WEEK

Celebrating the seasons of change

In Fall, the once-vibrant leaves that shimmered in the Summer sunlight, begin to change colour with the cooling earth. One by one, they turn to yellow, gold and brown, and finally, brilliant red. In the full blush of their splendor, they softly let go and drop to the earth.

As it is with the trees, it is with us, dear butterfly. For we each turn around with the seasons, and despite adversity, loss, and grief, we come around again in full bloom when the earth is warm with desire, and hope is once again alive in our bosom.

Living with grace comes through hope being at our helm, not fear. For as we know that the earth's gravity keeps us from being hurled out into space, and that the moon cradles us softly in her arms each night when it is time to rest, we must also remember that even in the coldest days of solitude, we can warm ourselves with the remembrances of Summers past, and our dreams for Summers future.

Lock door to sexual tumbleweeds

In desert, there is a strange plant that lives low to ground.

It get by on whatever come its way. It cares not to grow rich roots that would connect it to the earth, nor does it desire fragrant blossoms. Its colour matches the sparse brown landscape of the dusty plains. All the rain in the world will not make it bear fruit, nor tether it to the ground. Tumbleweeds live in the land of the coyote, rattlesnake, and prickly cactus.

Some men are like tumbleweeds. They appear at your door, empty handed, with nothing but a heart-breaking smile. Their shoes are worn and dusty from their travels. If you are prepared to let them warm themselves at your hearth for an evening or two, then let them in.

But do not make a place for them in your heart, for they will be carried with the wind before the summer harvest.

He who has blisters on feet, has song in heart

My dearest friend Mei Tai was a beautiful dancer. People would travel from far and near to see her famous fan dance, and she was agile as the tiger and gracious as the dove. Her body would move as if it had no laws of gravity acting against it.

One night, while attending one of her performances, I felt a quiet cloud of envy pass over me when she took a curtain bow. I felt like a sulking child when young men rushed over with roses, wanting her autograph. After the performance, I waited amid her admirers with a sour expression on my face. We walked back to her dressing room where I silently helped her out of her costume.

A wave of guilt passed over me for my unkind thoughts, as she gave me the biggest hug, with eyes rimmed in tears.

Wanting to open my heart to her and share my darkest thoughts, she slumped to the corner and unwrapped her toe shoes.

Have you ever noticed the dancer's feet?

The same feet that support the lovely pirouette, were bandaged from blisters. They were swollen, and red, and pained, yet they were beautiful and dazzling and lived in.

I never envied her after that, I only understood.

Reclaim virginity for ten thousandth time

When I was a young girl of eighteen, I received my first black sash in ancient art of Wu Shu. To receive that sash, students went through white or beginner's sash, then yellow, blue, red, brown and finally, black sash. According to my master, the great Yip Fung Dao, white symbolizes purity, while yellow, the dawn of new wisdom. Blue symbolizes hopes and ideals as high as sky, while red symbolizes the blood of battle. Brown symbolizes the richness of the earth, while black symbolizes the deep well of understanding that comes from all colours blending together.

As time pass, and I trained hard in broadsword and butterfly kick, my belt began to change. Little by little colour began to fade, and before my 25th year, belt looked white again. My master smiled at my distress, saying I was ready for another round of knowledge. I was pure again, and ready to re-learn my lessons from a new perspective.

When I was 50 years young, this happened again as life took on a deeper meaning. Master Dao say I should have the wisdom of the old master, but keep the heart of a young girl. Look into the mirror, Butterfly.

Are you not the young girl behind the silver hair?

If you feel worn and jaded, you are living at the edge of

yourself. That part is like a leaf in the wind, tossed about by every social calamity and storm. It becomes hardened with the seasons.

Life lived from the center part of ourselves is ever renewing and youthful.

Beware of dyslexic accountants

*O*nce upon a time there lived a successful accountant named Stanley Chew. Mr. Chew was associate in famous law firm, Trickster, Dollarhide, and Shmendrick. Mr. Chew had a reputation as being the best accountant on Mott street.

He so good, that all the big shots from Uptown and Wall Street sent their tax returns to him. (Mr. Chew was wizard at turning back the monetary odometer that the IRS love to run up.)

Mr. Chew had a beautiful secretary named Way Lee Wong. She made espresso for him each morning and handled prickly clients with great decorum.

Mr. Chew adored Way Lee. In fact, he adored her ample bosom, long black hair, and short skirts (which she wore to entice Mr. Chew).

One day, when he could stand it no longer, Mr. Chew make pass at Way Lee. That night, they began having an affair.

Soon, Mr. Chew began coming home later and later, with lipstick on collar (and even his boxer shorts).

Mrs. Chew smell a rat and began to spy on him through a telescope from stairwell of an adjacent building.

At first, it look like Way Lee was a hard working girl. (Mrs. Chew see Way Lee at Mr. Chew's desk, using his computer for more than half the day, while he was out running errands.)

Just as Mrs. Chew think she make mistake, her husband began to kiss his secretary passionately on his desk.

That night, amid waves of protests, Mr. Chew's wife demanded that Way Lee be fired.

Two weeks after Way Lee got her walking papers, Mr. Chew's bosses, Mr. Dollarhide and Mr. Shmendrick, called a meeting.

They wanted Mr. Chew to explain why his clients tax returns were messed up (the phone had been ringing off wall with irate clients).

Mr. Dollarhide showed Mr. Chew a return and demanded he fix errors. It seem all the numbers were reversed.

Instead of owing the IRS $19,000 dollars, one client was billed $91,000. Instead of fixing return, Mr. Chew rushed out of the office like a prisoner running from a firing squad.

After hours of downing Mimosas at Beaver's Palace, (a tawdry strip joint on Broadway), Mr. Chew came back to tell partners truth.

Mr. Chew say he is dyslexic, and it was Way Lee who corrected his returns before they went out to clients.

Madam Wong's advice is to learn from Stanley Chew, and never give authority a "blank check."

Zsu Yen was a lovely young woman with her eyes firm-ly set on the future. Each night she sat before the gilded mirror, combed her long black hair and dreamed of the perfect husband who would rescue her from her mundane world. Suitors admired her from afar, as she strolled listlessly amid the roses. But few dared to call on her, fearing they could not measure up to the men whom she had already dismissed.

Zsu Yen was a girl with many talents, including calligra-phy and sewing. She thought picking one would com-promise her options, so she chose nothing.

Years went by, and Zsu Yen's hair turned the colour of gently falling snow. She decided it was time to marry. Her first choice, Tie Yim, was now a fat and happy grandfather living in the country. She found that the second candidate, Sam Fung, died in a boating acci-dent ten years earlier.

Deciding marriage might not be the answer after all, she resumed sewing, which she had learned from her mother so many years ago. Arthritis made it painful to work with her hands, which trembled when she tried to patch a quilt. Besides, her eyesight had diminished to the point where she could not even thread a needle.

Zsu Yen spent the last winter of her life in bed, staring out at the leafless trees in the Summer garden, dreaming of her youth.

*He who lie low while enemy attacks,
sometime saves head*

When the stench of battle is upon you, it is best to squat down behind a large rock to tell from which direction the carnage is approaching. Take a look to see how many are in the party, and what game they are after.

If you are in the workplace, and bloodletting is under way, your best defense is to be like a shadow...quiet, and invisible. Some folks try to get close to the hand that wields the sword, but they might find their head on chopping block because the advancing army is like a school of sharks, attacking anything that moves.

If you are already emotionally wounded, do not show it, for they will smell the blood and begin to circle you. You could then take more strikes from co-workers caught up in the frenzy.

Sometime you may be subjected to abuse because others are jealous.

Be patient; it is better to let things roll off back than to lose energy defending your position.

If your boss is angry because your acceptance to art school means you can't work overtime, that is his problem. You got what you wanted, and that is all that counts. Co-workers are not family, so it doesn't matter what they think.

If you don't react, the sharks should soon circle some-one else.

But IF it appear that you have been targeted and they are out for the kill, lie low until you have a clear cut fighting plan. Do not get up and wave dagger in air to show the approaching assassins your tactical bag of tricks.

Lie in wait, with your psychological weaponry hidden beneath your cloak.

If you fight, use twice the power and cleverness the enemy has.

You must catch him off his feet.

Offer the enemy tea, and IF he begins to unsheathe sword, decapitate him as swiftly as possible.

Strike the mortal blow, and then quietly toast the vic-tory.

No need to gloat to co-workers as they place your Boss's severed head atop your work station.

Enjoy the victory quietly, and with grace.

Stand nude in front of mirror

Stand nude in front of mirror, Butterfly. Tell me, what do you see? Rejoice first in the things that you love most. Is it your hair that falls softly on your shoulders, or your eyes that are large and luminous.

Look again at what YOU think are imperfections. (Hips that may be larger than your best friend, whom you secretly envy.)

If hips are too large from sedentary lifestyle and junk food, discipline yourself to make the change.

If you have taken all measures in attaining your ideal goal, and body stands firm in retaining its form, then accept the differences the creator has given you.

Look again at hips. Are they not strong and steady? Maybe you are built more like plow horse than race horse. But plow horse can stand firm and steady under summer sun and work the fields without dropping.

Is that not beauty?

If whistle blow, get off track

Those who walk past the abandoned tin factory by the slippery slope of the river bank can see an old, legless man sitting beside the railroad tracks. It has been this way since my mother brought me to the river's edge when I was no higher than newly-planted bamboo. Many years ago, the old man, Tzo Tse, was a young man of twenty with a strong body and dark, brooding eyes.

I thought to myself, "I will grow up and be so beautiful that he will take his eyes off the train tracks and come up to marry me." But he did not.

My mother told me Tzo Tse was born in an old shack where the train now runs. While he was away in the military fighting, his parents died, and the shack was torn down. When he returned, he could not accept the loss. One day, he cursed and waved his fist too close to an oncoming train, which took off his right hand. Not long after, he lost a leg, and then another foot. Each evening at twilight, the townspeople carry food down by the river bank. Tzo Tse hobbles on his stumps to the river's edge where he eats alone. Every evening he sleeps under a gnarled lemon tree.

When we lay our body across path of danger should we curse the heavens?

Even most beautiful butterfly began as caterpillar

Long ago, a fuzzy brown caterpillar lived among the spiders and squirrels on the branches of an old juniper tree. Mr. Caterpillar felt sad as he watched a family of red spiders spin their intricate web. He sighed at the way they created a beautiful tapestry from deep within themselves, and wondered what hidden talents he might have. The youngest spiders made fun of him as he slowly passed by, fearful of the long drop down.

They said he was a "big fat glob of nothing."

Fall was approaching, and the weather was no longer his friend.

A family of squirrels began to collect nuts for the winter, and add an extra layer of leaves to their nest. Mr. Caterpillar was feeling so cold and lonely that he didn't know what to do. Crawling to the lowest branches of the evergreen, he hid his face and began to cry.

His tears turned to silk, which became a blanket that shielded him from the harsh north winds. Layer upon layer of his tears created a cocoon which surrounded him during the winter snows. He drifted in and out of consciousness, and felt alone in his dark world. "Is this all my life is meant to be?," he sighed, as he heard the laughter from the squirrels scampering across the branches.

Weeks went by, until the warmth from the spring sunlight rekindled a desire deep within him. No longer to be contained in the small area which was once his solace, he began to twist and pull to squeeze himself out of its grip.

"Something terrible has happened," he cried as he tried to crawl onto the branch. He only had two feet! A gust of wind knocked him frontward and he fell off the branch. A few feet from the ground Mr. Caterpillar was miraculously saved by a beautiful creature with golden wings. It floated him to safety to the edge of a clear pond.

Wanting to thank the strange creature, he looked down and cried in delight when he saw his own image reflected in the clear pond.

Mr. Caterpillar realized he was now a butterfly, and that the beautiful creature was himself!

The minute the conversation starts, they make a straight thrust to your psyche. You feel like you are on witness stand instead of engaged in a mutual exchange of thoughts and feelings. Like an octopus spraying black ink, they spew out arrogant, judgmental statements to keep you moving backward and from seeing who they are.

You play into their hands if you move back, blocking their insults and prying questions with endless explanations. Tao say to move aside from this person and let him pass.

Then you will see that he is only a beggar putting a price on the gold sandals you wear on your feet.

Should I marry him, Madam Wong?

Years ago, while my sister's daughter, Woo Shin and I were preparing tea for some visiting cousins, Woo Shin ask me, "Madam Wong, should I marry Sammy Lee?"

This handsome young man came from a good family, was at the university studying law, and had impeccable manners. I tell her the outside look good, but she should ask herself the following question:

Is he a man, or is he a boy? Her answers were all about his external gifts, (He look great in bikini swim suit and know how to pick best restaurants in town). I tell her it is great he understand how to invest in stocks, and good at the fox trot, but is he a man?

I offered the same guidelines my grandmother gave to me:

A boy fears and tries to hide it. A man expresses his fears and pushes onward.

A boy needs a woman to be his mother. A man wants a woman to be an equal.

A boy likes to act like he is always in control; A man knows he has a lot to learn from a woman, and is not afraid of sharing his feelings, or the power it appears to give her.

A boy needs to compartmentalize women, so one isn't valued too much, or fills too many needs. A man wants a whole friendship, and values other avenues than sex.

A boy builds walls and blames others for his pain. A man welcomes his fear, knowing it has come for a reason, and asks the universe to teach him the lessons hidden within the pain.

A boy says he isn't ready to let go and trust because it is easier to stay a hurt child. A man welcomes the opportunity and cherishes a woman who is patient, loving and, yes, imperfect.

Now Woo Shin, I ask her, "Are you a girl, or are you a woman?" If you are both adults, I would say yes to marriage. If not, you are merely playing house, wearing shoes that are too big to walk in.

Leave emotional black holes to astronomers

Looking up at the heavens on a cloudless night, you can see the beautiful stars shimmering like precious diamonds. The light radiating from the twinkling stars travels millions and millions of miles to reach us.

Some people are like that. They radiate love, wisdom, and warmth.

Others are like black holes that suck in the life force from their environment and give nothing in return. They are dead at center, where a vacuum exists. Like a bucket with a hole in it, love from others is received, but drips out of bottom, so that no satisfaction point is ever reached. These people feel empty and alone and are always hungry. But they can be treacherous beneath their sorrowful eyes, because they can pull you into their gravitational field through guilt and pity.

It is our destiny to stand separate from others and create our own light from within.

This we can share with others and bask in the healing love that is always around us.

Then we can take our rightful place in the most precious wonders of creations, the human constellation.

Puritanism and pornography are opposite sides of same coin

When Wa Shin and I first went to picture show in America, it was 1944. Most movies were war stories or romantic comedies that showed men and women in a positive light. You could say, movies had a lot of heart.

As decades passed, movies changed a lot.

I remember Wa Shin and I walking home from a Greenwich Village theater in 1975. We didn't like the movie we had seen because it was shallow and violent. Although no one was in love, there was a lot of sex. It seem as women gain power in society, she lose it on film. Women's roles are often cold, aggressive and sexually insatiable.

Wa Shin and I wondered is that what American men think of women?

Male roles are not any better. Filmmakers reduce men to de-humanized killing machines.

Love and integrity have been exchanged for casual sex and violence.

How did sex get so disconnected from the heart?

Many people have casual sex because they are afraid of really connecting with another person. How easy it is for them to take off their clothes with a stranger, rather than be "seen" emotionally by someone else.

Puritans are afraid of showing their bodies and feeling pleasure in them, while pornographers fear connecting with another person emotionally.

Without heart, sex is not making love. It is a bodily function that has no more meaning than changing tire on car or taking out the trash.

Without heart, filmmaker produces junk because eye is only on profit.

Without heart, teacher cannot teach, mother cannot mother.

Without heart, there is nothing.

When to fight and went to say Master Card or Visa?

All the muscle in the world will do no good if you have no brain. There is a time to fight and a time to compromise.

If someone is trying to kill you, you MUST fight...there is no other choice.

If a mugger is high on crack waving gun in search of money for fix, it is better to open your purse and give him what he wants, doing so with a calm, quiet voice.

But if mugger is a coward, looking for an 'easy mark', it is better to 'jump-punch him,' or confront him BEFORE anything happens.

When I was in my thirties, my mother visited us in New York.

Leaving the restaurant, a "low life" began to follow us.

I told Mother to hurry back to restaurant and get Wa Shin.

Walking up to bully, I tell him if he mess with my family he will be spitting out teeth on way to emergency room.

I grabbed a beer bottle lying in the alley and broke the top off of it, while I moved into a Cat stance

(To be honest, now I might even say, "Make my day, ass hole.")

The dirt bag saw I meant business, and ran down the street.

Always let your first instinct be your guide. If you are being followed, never isolate yourself.

If you feel mugger is crazy or has a weapon, use your calmness and clever mind.

If a man wielding a bloody ax breaks down door and stares at you with his wild, demented eyes, you can, in order of preference:

1. Pull out a .357 magnum and make a Jackson Pollack painting out of living room wall.

2. Escape through a bathroom window.

3. Say lovingly, "You look a bit tired. Could I fix you some Jasmine tea?"

Most muggers are weak cowards, but if you look into the eyes of a very desperate and angry man, slowly pull out your wallet and say, "Master Card or Visa?"

*Even those who ride the crest of youth
have to come ashore sometime*

Youth is a vibrant, giddy time when the young stand in unison, singing the same song with the same voice.

Locking arms in solidarity of their newly-found adulthood, the young come ashore.

"We have arrived," is their battle cry. Everything is new and wondrous, to be tried and experienced!

And it is good.

But God never gives all gifts or trials to one age group, and so it is with the young. For along with the lineless face, and muscular frame, comes a tabula rasa, or unlived life. What will be written on it, through fate and endeavor, is up to us.

Once we come ashore, we begin to scatter like leaves in the wind. Some stay close to shore, afraid to venture onward to create their own unique destiny. Like aging Peter Pans, they create a illusionary world where they are perpetually in their twenties. They never mature emotionally, and gather the knowledge and life experience to pass to those who come ashore behind them.

Others get bogged down in a marsh of disillusionment and disappointment when life etches its first painful mark on the once flawless face.

Some make it to a small pond that over the years

becomes stagnant, when fresh ideas and courage are dammed up by self-satisfaction.

But some journey until they find fresh waters at the source of life. They travel like salmon, upstream, against the currents to forge their own unique destiny. Youth is God's gift to us. What we do with it is our gift to God.

If you are with loser, what wrong with you?

Gerta Lee was one of the most difficult clients who came to store for herbal remedy. Her eyes were like small raisins, glaring out from underneath a rancid scarf which was worn well past its prime. She shuffled as though she were on her last leg, and seemed to delight with the latest details of her phlebitis and chronic constipation. Mostly, she liked to recount the sordid details of her unhappy life with Sam Lee.

Gerta say her problem started when she gave up a dancing career to marry the bold Sam Lee, a part-time banker and full-time racketeer.

Gerta say on their first date, Sam picked her up with breath so saturated with gin that one match would have set the whole town in flames. Still, he had a large wallet and a gleam in his eye, so Gerta looked the other way.

It wasn't long until she had four children and a drawer full of bills. Sam Lee spent time in and out of jail, picked up for urinating on the mayor's front lawn.

Gerta always claim that if it hadn't been for Sam Lee, she would have led an illustrious life as a dancer and would have married the perfect man.

Last year, her youngest child offered to let her live with him, but Gerta declined, saying it wouldn't be right to leave Sam Lee when he needed her most. Dr. Zen offered to operate on Gerta's leg, free of charge, so that she could be cured of her chronic limp.

She declined the offer, saying it wouldn't be right to take charity.

One of Gerta's classmates, Shu Shu Tie, was picking out red onions when Gerta was recounting how she brought the house down with her performance as Juliet in the famous ballet. "Funny," Shu Shu told me, as she brought the onions to the counter, "I attended that performance and vividly remember that Gerta was seated in the audience three rows down from me."

A roach is a roach by any other name

Madam Wong hear certain things over and over from young girls whose hearts have been broken by a "man who couldn't help himself." He may speak these words in the early stages of courtship, before going to bed with her, or after she is three months pregnant. But be assured, dear one, when a man reads you his 'romantic disclaimer,' take it seriously, because his heart and soul are already out the door.

He is telling you he will not be held responsible for breaking your heart. (Meaning he probably will, and the disclaimer is his way of disowning guilt).

Romantic disclaimers always begin with "I don't want to hurt you, but..."

I don't want to hurt you, but...

> I am not ready for a serious relationship
> I am not over my last love
> I want to date around
> I am too young for marriage
> I am married
> I am in medical school,
> or...

I want someone younger
I always wanted a Jewish
girl
am more attracted to your
brother
I'm off to an Ashram

If you hear your man sing this tune, it is best to polite-
ly excuse yourself, find a can of insect repellent under
the sink and demand that he leave at once.

This romantic roach is selfish and cruel because he
thinks by giving you his disclaimer, ("I told you I wasn't
ready for marriage four years ago") that he has not
done anything wrong.

Some men play this game their whole life because naive
girls believe love will turn an insect into a king.

Emotions like rooster on weather vane,
always changing

One day, we feel like we're on highest mountain top. Another day, we view world from a dark abyss of gloom and despair. One day, we can fight tiger with one hand behind our back, and another day we feel like a frightened church mouse, scurrying to escape the heavy steps of Father Fear.

Some people work very hard to pretend they are in control of their thoughts and feelings. The truth is, our feelings are often as changeable as the weather.

As sure as we are basking in life's golden bounty, we know that fall will come, and with it, the passing of things and people we held dear to our heart.

Life is easier when we accept and understand that change is an inescapable process of all creation.

When we feel a storm of emotion approaching, we can take shelter at the center of ourselves.

The deepest part of ourselves is quiet, vast, and unchanging. We can acknowledge that outside, on the "personality" part of ourselves, a tornado whirls by. When we silently pray for quiet and peace, we can ride out storm behind the shelter of our soul.

Are you a snake charmer?

Anger, like other "negative emotions" gets an unfair reputation.

Culture implies anger is like a deadly cobra that should be kept in the closet. No one wish to stir their sleeping serpent. (We secretly hope it has slithered off to neighbor's house, and has happily taken up residence there.) Yet no part of us can remain hidden forever.

We smile and smile as snake slithers underneath door and up our chair. We even take snake under our shirt to hide from world, until snake turns on master and bites. We end up with ulcers, cancer, and high blood pressure. Can you learn to be a snake charmer? Can you learn to entice anger and its brother, jealousy out of hiding?

Say to snake as its head is fanned out undulating to music: "Oh powerful one, what is the message behind your dance?"

At first, the viper might strike a time or two, but if you persist, the snake will begin to share its masked grief. As you pass through anger's protective wall of fire, you can rescue parts of self that have been held hostage by your rage.

In time, you can become a master snake charmer. You can learn to transform anger into peace and understanding.

As snake becomes friend, it will stretch out like a bridge for you to travel to the most primitive parts of yourself, returning with your lost treasures.

Even prisoner of pain can ask for pardon

All of us have done things we aren't proud of, and so it was with Sam Tie. As a former prisoner of war, he survived many things in life: three years internment in a Japanese camp, the death of his best friend and cell mate, and the disappearance of his father while Sam was away at war.

Mr. Tie learned to survive by seat of pants. He learn how to recover socks off dead man before rigor mortis set in. The same socks help keep him from freezing to death when winter set in. Mr. Tie learned to will his mind into turning a few tablespoons of rice into nourishing food, vowing through clenched fist, that he would not be defeated.

Mr. Tie later returned from war, promising to put it behind him.

But despite success - a thriving business, and loving family - Sam began to have a drinking condition. He began to shut out loved ones through mean talk and strong drink. Everyone think it was war that drove Sam into his melancholic fits.

What Sam never talk about, was the death of his baby brother.

When Sam was nine years old, he was playing ball at the river's edge with his baby brother. Sam, accidentally threw the ball into the river and went out to retrieve it. His brother followed him into the river and was swept away by the swift current.

At funeral, mother blamed Sam for his brother's death. Sam was able to walk away from prison cell, but not from his spiritual internment. Sam was imprisoned by his mother's guilt. His mother drown her living son's soul and stabbed him in heart with shame daggers.

Sam's suffering was much harder and crueler than his baby brother, for little brother's life ended quickly, while Sam died a little each day.

One evening, while attending to Sam's recurring bouts of delirium from malaria, I whisper to Sam that I am his long lost brother. I tell him I am happy and content, and beg him to leave his prison of pain and let his heart run free. I tell him that mother regret what she say and she love him dearly. I tell him to love others as he would have loved us.

In my nightly prayers, I shut eyes and see Sam Tie leaving his prison of pain as he moves into the light of forgiveness and love.

Tell me, who needs your prayers of love and hope?

Let those in need receive your love with an open heart.

Shedding the old skins of ourselves with grace

Sometimes we glide through life with ease, feeling comfortable with ourselves and with others. These are the times when we are growing into our spiritual skins.

Then something happen and life becomes uncomfortable, like a set of clothing that is too tight.

It could be that nothing around us changes except our perspective.

This is time when we are outgrowing our spiritual skins.

Nine months after conception, baby has grown too big for the space it occupies inside mother.

World seem to be pushing in on baby from all directions. Its home collapses while it is pushed down a narrow hallway which is squeezing and screaming.

Through whole process, baby is terrified and angry.

Yet baby survives and grows to adulthood!

Through life we experience a series of births and deaths.

Some are easy to spot, like onset of puberty, pregnancy, and menopause.

Emotional rights of passages are endless:

A ten-year-old has to deal with jealousy and guilt when she learns about new baby brother.

A very beautiful woman has to come to terms with aging and losing youth.

A wealthy man and pillar of community has to redefine himself after he loses fortune.

Our soul continues to have its own births and deaths throughout our life.

During that time we experience the same emotions we had during labor: Fear, Anger, Grief, Vulnerability.

It is often a time when we are painfully self-conscious, because we are not sure who we are.

The time we are most uncomfortable means we are on the threshold of breaking through to a greater place.

Where we once felt strong and powerful, we feel weak, and vulnerable, like newborn.

As you see your former self lying in corner like a heap of ashes, do not judge it harshly, for it was once a vital part of you. It was sloughed off like a butterfly's cocoon when it became too tight, and your new being underneath the death and decay was ready for birthing.

Rejoice both the death and the rebirth, for both are needed in your life journey.

Do not curse cloud which hide you from man-eating tiger

Tie Yim was a thirty-year old warrior who had a secret. Each night in dream he would hear the strange sound of a creature behind dark swirling fog, that would roll in as his heart pounded in terror. What lay behind that black fog Mr. Yim not know.

For years he wished to know the answer behind the riddle that kept him from feeling the inner confidence that would mirror the outer reflection of grace and power. In dream sometime he would curse the fog, demanding that it reveal to him this terrible demon of the night, so he could confront it, once and for all, and slay it with his broad sword. Each night before sleeping, he would demand that an answer be given to him in his dreams. But the harder he demanded, the thicker the fog became, until he could no longer even hear the monster but could only feel its presence.

One day he could no longer stand the torture of not knowing and began to cry. On his knees he prayed. Instead of hating the monster, he began to pray for it. He began to accept its presence and even wish it no harm. He no longer cared if it ate him.

In his dream the fog began to clear. At first he saw a green dragon with fiery eyes and a darting tongue. As he approached the dragon with love instead of fear, the dragon began to melt.

Behind it was the mask of a man with an arrogant and rigid expression. As Mr. Yim look closer, he cried, seeing that the face was his own. His tears of recognition melted the mask, which turned into a small white dove that fluttered its wings and gently flew towards the sun.

He who chews cud all day, not hungry at dinner

Some people are like cows. They spend their day eating a little here, a little there. They are never really hungry, yet never really full. Just sort of in between. When it comes time to sit down for life's banquet, they can only take in a few bites.

Some expend their creative energy chattering indiscriminately. By the time they sit down to work, they have little energy left. Many Westerners spend a great deal of time polishing an image, so energy is spent on outside ego creation instead of their authentic being. Behind super-macho, "nothing bother me" image is a frightened child, afraid to reveal real self. Instead of watering the plant, they water the pot. No wonder plant not grow.

Others expend energy talking about how bad things are in the world, yet when given an opportunity to do something to change it, they decline, believing that their actionless "thoughts" were, in themselves, enough.

What will you do with your physical, spiritual, and creative force? Will you nourish it until it reaches maturity, so you can share it with the world? Or will you let your juices spill on the ground indiscriminately, in little dribbles here and there, so that in the end, there is nothing?

What to do about romantic tar babies

Over years, Madam Wong hear same story. It go like this:

Young woman (or her mother) come to store with swollen eyes and an aching heart. This girl in love with man who can't give her what she want. She know it, yet she feels stuck to him. In fact, she want him even more. (Once she wraps her legs around him during a night of merry-making, she stuck to him like he was a tar baby.) Most people mistakenly think that problem lie with their particular "romantic tar baby." This not so.

From my experience, woman will come back a year later with a new "romantic tar baby." (A different name and face, with the same emotional profile.)

Girl love romantic tar baby because unconsciously, it remind her of similar feelings she had with her father. If she can't win father's love, she will attract another man who is unavailable or hurtful and will try again.

Deep in heart, she feel if she win with tar baby, she win double: She gets tar baby to love her, and unconsciously heals the past and wins father's love.

Solution not lie in man but in woman.

Question is not, "How can I get man to love me?", but "Why don't I believe I am worthy of being loved?"

When you no longer NEED to grovel for romantic table

scraps, you will be able to unhook from tar baby.

Don't blame self, Butterfly, if your wings are stuck to unworthy man. You are trying to unfree self, but only can do so when you learn the lesson in the pain.

That day, you can unstick wings and fly off.

Always remember, it is not man you are stuck to, but LESSON about yourself that you have to learn. Tar baby is there to help you grow and move on so you can later get what you really want and deserve.

Let silence not be a scepter to rule over others

When I was young, my best friend was Mae San, a lovely, quiet girl with dark eyes and pale skin. She was delicate and rare like an orchid, who needed protection from the harsh social winds. A rare orchid which needed just the right amount of light and humidity. There were always attendants to admire her lovely petals and provide her with sunlight and rain.

In years we knew each other, until her death, I never saw her cry. I never saw her fall madly in love, or feel hate or great joy or sorrow.

I was one of her attendants who protected her from overzealous admirers whom she had tired of.

When I was eighteen, Wa Shin and I married. After children came, Mae San's path and mine went in separate directions.

Once while we visited in market, she told me quietly that I had outgrown her. She said she missed me, yet never made an effort to renew friendship.

When I began to reexamine friendship, I saw that mine had been the active part, and hers the passive. I began to see her less as an orchid, and more as a Queen bee. She lay there, holding court, expecting her social drones to do all the work. Her beauty and feigned frailty was all she thought she needed. If we did something she did not like, Mae San would retreat to her room with one of her headaches and not emerge for hours.

I did not realize the power that behavior had over me. I did not understand that her silence was a scepter she ruled over others. We danced to her silent tune throughout our lives, until her suicide at thirty-five.

It seemed sad that I never saw the deepest parts of her.

I sensed it at times, but I never really saw it.

If I had the courage and understanding, I would have gently confronted her. I would have expected more out of her, and would not have paid homage to the dummy self that she propped up alongside her bed, and would not have settled until the real Mae San crept out from behind the mask.

The night Mae San die, she appeared to me in a dream. Dressed in a white gown, she stood behind a gold gate, which rose unattached in a field of wheat. The sky was dark blue and the stars were shimmering like diamonds. She told me to promise to give the following words to her parents:

Ode to the living
(Mae San's song)

In the stillness of the morn, weep not
For the future left unborn, weep not
Weep not, the golden days of Summer
Or the passing of Autumn's fragrant leaves
Or the oak, cut down in all its splendor
Amid the tender shade of loving trees.

Speak not, "I could haves", or "If onlys."
Wear not the bitter bridle of loves guilt
Be not the grim reaper of the lonely,
Or wrap up thyself in life's dark melancholy cloak.

Drink from the cool waters of forgiveness
And eat from the fruit of everlasting love
Leave footprints in the sand that are endless
Live, laugh, and remember, with the unencumbered peace of the dove.

Emotional abuse sometime worse than blow to face

When I began martial art training, I found out how it feel to get hit in face. How it hurt to train body to do knuckle, wrist, and even finger tip push ups on bare wooden floor. I learned how to take a blow to stomach, by doing five-hundred sit ups.

I remember what it felt like when a two hundred and twenty pound man accidentally hit me in head with a spinning heel kick. I floated to the floor in a trance-like state, observing with detachment, the look of concern on my teacher's face.

In time, my bruises healed, and I learned a lot.

I learned to transcend physical pain to achieve a goal. Body is a miraculous thing. It heals by creating new skin, and bone. But healing the heart is not so easy when the spirit is pierced through by cruel, hateful talk from others. What child ever forgets the face of its mother or father, who says he or she is no good? What child heals from being humiliated and shamed, and blamed for things they were not even responsible for, or were too young to understand?

So many adults do bad things because they have low self image. Most narcissists puff themselves up because they believe they have to appear perfect to be accepted.

Why? They fear they will not be accepted unless they are better than others. They feel they have to EARN the right to exist.

Think before you speak, dear one. Your words wound deeper than any sword, and leave a mark the depths of which only God can see.

What to do when man exposes himself on subway

When I was visiting my darling granddaughter Shin Lee, at her dorm at NYU, I had the delightful opportunity to see what a brave and courageous young girl she was. And it made my heart sing!

Here is what little Shin Shin did when a man made an improper pass at her on subway:

Shin Shin say while on the southbound A train to Wall Street, an attractive well-dressed man with a brief case stood behind her.

As subway took off, she began to feel a unusual rhythm coming from the man directly behind her. Movement came from first Chakra area (between mans legs!) Shin Shin say she couldn't believe what she must be feeling. She looked down and noticed the mans feet were on either side of hers. She could not confirm the source of problem because train was too crowded.

As train slow down at Canal Street, and passengers began to exit, Shin Shin look down and saw, bigger than life, that Mr. Businessman had an erection.

Instead of being a victim to this abuse, Shin Shin say to man in loud voice:

"Excuse me sir, but I see you have an erection. Perhaps you should visit the men's room to relieve yourself of this condition."

Everyone began to stare at Mr. Businessman. As clod hurried to get off train, he covered up his groin with a briefcase.
Shin Shin followed behind him and yelled,
"Look Out For The Man With An Erection!"

Shin Shin was still angry over situation as she recounted the tale in her cramped apartment while I poured Jasmine tea. But I told her that she parried his sexual attack with the grace of an Aikido master, by putting the focus of shame back on him. She took control of an upsetting situation where he counted on her to be passive, and too embarrassed to speak up.
Shin Shin know not to take blame for something someone else does, so she felt free to speak up, and defend herself by letting the world know what a clod Mr. Businessman was.
Don't let someone play you for a fool. If someone does something improper (like putting a hand on your leg in a crowded movie theater), scream out,
"You Have Thirty Seconds To Get Hand Off My Thigh, Before I Kick Your Sleazy Ass."
I tell you Butterfly, that snake will slither off in grass and look for a more willing victim.

Mind like tea bag, what ever it steep in, it taste like

Think about the friends you have in your life now. Are they kind, caring and honest? Do they respect your thoughts and feelings?

Can they be counted on when you are in trouble? If your friends are wonderful, then you are in proper atmosphere.

If your friends are hateful and mean, or if they lie and take advantage of you or others, what are you doing with them?

Could it be that part of their ugly behavior attracts you?

If you are suffering in unhappy relationships, ask self what need you have for them in life?

(To live out martyr fantasy, or to finally hit bottom and realize you deserve better treatment.)

They must serve some purpose or they would not there. Be honest with yourself. It is only from true self disclosure that change can be made.

If you are unhappy, let go of relationships that are no longer fulfilling while you visualize what you really want. Begin to act in way that you want to be treated. You are in control of your life. You have to take responsibility for the relationships in your life. If you don't like what is there, let it go, and strive to be the kind of person who deserves better. Don't allow negativity to take you down. Walk away from disappointments and behavior that is unpleasant to you.

Wish the best for yourself and others, knowing that water does seek its own level.

TV like too many face lifts...give face a vacant look

In America, many young children and adults spend as much as thirty hours a week sitting in front of TV. Imagine how many brain cells die while bored, unhappy person eats potato chips and cheese whiz while watching soap opera and cop-and-robber show.

I never hear of culture that can thrive when living takes a back seat to watching.

When I was a young girl, I heard a terrible story of a doctor who was accidentally locked up in mental ward for the chronically ill. She was surrounded by psychotic patients twenty four hours a day.

A year passed, and by the time mistake had been cleared up, woman doctor goofy as a one-eyed possum. American version of "Chinese Water Torture" is game show. When watching, what are you doing to enhance your body, mind, and spirit?

Each day you should be able to name something new you learn.

Ask yourself what good deed you did for someone else.

Each week, plan something you have never done, and try to do something you never have had the courage to do.

Use discipline when watching TV, eating ice cream, or buying expensive clothes.

Everything in moderation.

Jealousy is the soup that feeds the malnourished

In a seaside cliff near Pu Dang Province, lives an old, broken woman the townspeople call, "woman of rags." Thirty years ago, she was a handsome woman with many suitors who called on her at her mansion on the hill.

She never worked in life, only had special fittings for silk dresses, commissioned artists to paint her portrait, and gave lavish dinner parties. Despite wealth, Lee Sin never felt satisfied. If she gave a party and another woman wore a prettier dress, Lee Sin fired dressmaker and, in fit of anger, ripped up all her clothes and threw in gutter.

One day, she fell in love with a famous doctor who had a daughter.

Lee Sin try very hard to place daughter in a private school, far from Quingdao Province, so she could have father all to herself.

In front of daughter, Lee Sin appeared cordial and pleasant, but underneath, she plotted to cause discord between father and daughter. Lee Sin even went so far as to intercept letters the daughter wrote to her father (which she tore up in a fit of jealousy).

Three years later the doctor died and left everything to his daughter. In a fit of rage, Lee Sin hired best attorneys to try to take over doctor's home.

Years passed, and Lee Sin spent thousands of dollars on appeals so she could force doctor's daughter to go through inheritance.

Finally, Lee Sin lose last appeal. Angry that she too had lost thousands of her own money in ugly legal dispute, she let a handsome, young stockbroker handle her financial affairs. The impetuous youth unwisely invested in Futures, while pocketing large amounts for trade commissions.

Within a few years, Lee Sin was bankrupt. Her only accomplishment in life had been spending money, so Lee Sin not know what to do. She took to drinking.

A few years later, her house was repossessed, and Lee Sin began to wander the streets aimlessly, wearing the black lace nightgown the doctor bought her.

During the day, Lee Sin looks for food scraps in trash dumps with the buzzards on She Do Pier. Townspeople say she is nuttier than a wharf rat. At midnight, she walks in the moonlight near the lighthouse where she can be seen dancing to imaginary music.

"Oh yes, Dr. Zan, I will marry you." Lee Sin say.

"And Dr. Zan, I am so sorry to hear about the death of your daughter. Drowning is such a terrible way to go. Perhaps a trip to France will lift your spirits. Caviar, Dr. Zan, ...some brandy, perhaps?"

Women should sweep floor with broom, not use for transportation

I don't believe modern women are as liberated as they would like to think. Every day, I meet sad, lost women who by Western standard, have everything; fancy job, good paycheck, and nice car.

These women come home at 10:00 p.m. to empty house and TV dinner (they are too modern to know how to cook). On dates, many want to open door for men and have sex with less discrimination (proving that Australopithecus is not extinct as some would believe).

Women are taught to "behave like a man in the corporate world." (Some women even wear ties, and feel black lace bras are a plot to keep them enslaved.)

The word "feminine" is a four letter word in some circles. It is not politically correct (along with mink coat, and French fries).

The idea that women and men are same goes against ten thousand years of evolution.

Today's women not understand what every other generation before her knew: that for romance and mating, polarity of the sexes is very important.

Women are keeper of the romantic flame. They ARE the home. It is a woman's loving nature and understanding of her own femininity that makes a man rush out to protect and take care of her.

It is woman's heart that keeps a man coming back to her bed - not just her body. Any man can pick up phone and get some silly girl to offer sex with no strings attached.

A woman's heart, mind and spirit is what makes her powerful.

She is the doorway to eternity, ushering in a new generation, as her mother and grandmother before.

While the men with testosterone poisoning are killing randomly throughout the world, in wars that should never have been, the women bear the children, sing their songs and create.

Tell me, is that not power?

Auto eroticism and romantic maintenance

For moment, think of your body as a beautiful car. It needs to be given the right fuel and periodic tune-ups to run properly. It is taken to car wash and to mechanic for repairs.

Now think of your body as a sensual, sexual machine. What happens when no proper suitor is around, and you are left without a lover?

Some women brag that they never "touch themselves" if boyfriend not around. I say to them, that car sitting too long in garage causes battery to run down, and when they get out on romantic highway they quickly run out of gas!

Besides, dear one, caring for your own needs is much better than feeling so frustrated that you cannot sit without wriggling.

Think of the kind of losers you attract with THOSE vibrations. (Remember, you are vulnerable to the Sexual Tumbleweed variety when you give off vibrations that only come from below the waist.)

You can practice tantric sexual techniques with your-self, and why not?

It will keep your sensuality alive, but in check.

When your new man gallops over the horizon and scoops you into his arms for an evening of romance, you will not handle his ardor as if it were a runaway garden hose, but the wonderful monument to procreation and virility that it is.

Even man with one testicle can still produce offspring

Once there was a young man name Yew Yang. Poor Yew was ugly as a mud fence. His eyes were slightly crossed, and he was so nearsighted that he once mistook a cactus for a soldier trying to hitch a ride on an Arizona highway. Yew was also the butt of locker room jokes because he only had one testicle.

Yew was studying to be an engineer at NYU. At a party, he met a lovely girl named Shu Lynn. That night, he walked her home after her date got drunk and passed out. It was love at first sight for Yew, but Shu wasn't interested in him romantically, so they became friends. Over the next few years, Shu dated some very handsome fraternity men, but nothing ever worked out.

One boyfriend, Larry Lee, would fall asleep before he picked her up on dates, because he was a triathlete and spent all his energy exercising.

Another boyfriend, Sammy Jay, had a roving eye, and made a pass at Shu's roommate. The third, Ivan Chumly, went to doctor for a sex change operation.

Through it all, Yew remained a loyal friend, and supported Shu through each heartbreak.

As time pass, Shu began to appreciate Yew more and more.

One night, over a glass of white wine, Shu ask Yew to make love to her.

The next morning while making breakfast for Yew, Shu realize that he had all the right qualities of a husband and father:

He was loyal, dedicated, kind, gentle, and hardworking.

Yew was so happy with Shu in bed, he decided not to "rock boat" and push for a commitment.

One month later, Shu proposed to Yew!!!

They were married by Justice of Peace during Spring Break.

Nine months later, Shu gave birth to a baby boy.

Relationship is like flower; without love it dry up

In great Southwest, there exists a land of magical beauty.

There is beauty in the starkness of nature.

Gigantic cliffs hold court over the rustic plains.

Eagles circle in the hushed silence of a hot summer's day.

From a distance, nothing seems as mighty and powerful as these mountains.

But there is something much more powerful.

Nearly hidden behind sage brush is a delicate channel that has cut its way through entire mountain.

Water dripping slowly over stone dissolves it.

Water...clear, fluid, boundless, formless, is one of the most powerful elements on earth.

Love is like water: It can change course when there is no direct route. It can be scorned or frozen and melts back to its original state, as it is forgiving. Water always finds a path, as love does. And love, like water, can melt even the hardest heart of stone, with a slow, steady drip of unconditional understanding and acceptance.

Love is silent and steady, and cannot be measured by yardsticks, or the five senses.

But it is real, and its power is behind all great acts of courage, creativity and greatness.

Spite like vomit, leave an aftertaste

Old man Chen Do lived next door to a large, noisy family with six children and three dogs. Mr. Do was a retired schoolteacher with a passion for gardening. He spent entire days weeding and planting his garden, hand picking tiny scraps of paper with minute care.

Mr. Do hated his noisy neighbors with a passion. He tried everything to get them to stop their nocturnal racket. He called police, and banged on door at 2:00 a.m. He even clang cymbals in children's window while they slept, as an act of revenge. Finally, next door neighbor agreed to keep children under rein and promised to keep noise down.

Mr. Do should have been happy to let matter drop. Instead, his resentment for neighbors grew.

Without the noise to focus on, and be a channel for his hatred, Mr. Do began to focus on dogs. Dogs not do much. They simply eat and take dump. Mr. Do began to plot their demise. He began to think of different ways to poison dogs. He settled on a plan to soak pork strips in a dangerous chemical, and feed to dogs.

One night, Mr. Do set out a container of poison on the patio, and marinated the pork. In the middle of night came a giant storm which dumped four inches of rain on town. The wind blew strongly, toppling over chairs and plant containers. Mr. Do forgot about the poison until he went outside for morning tea.

To his shock, Mr. Do found his entire garden dead. All the plants shriveled up, and the fruit dropped to the ground. A large gallon jug lay overturned, and the meat lay strewn out in the mud. Mr. Do's prized roses, which he planned to enter in a contest, lay shriveled alongside his white parakeet, Foo Foo.

That was the last time Mr. Do was hateful. He looked at storm as a warning from God.

That Spring, Mr. Do planted a new garden for himself and for his neighbors too. Neighbors so grateful, they began to invite Mr. Do over for dinner.

They found out that Mr. Do was very lonely and missed his wife, who died of a stroke. Neighbors found out Mr. Do's personality is like prickly cactus; thorny on outside, but sweet and gentle on inside.

Now Mr. Do has two passions: Gardening, and playing Grampa.

Intuition is an angel whispering in your ear

Madam Wong want to tell a story that she never told anyone in life except for best friend. She not even tell husband. She tell you this because she care for you and do not want you to make same mistake. Mistake caused lots of trauma, and could have cost Madam Wong her life.

While attending college in China, Madam Wong visited cousins in New York City for one month. One weekend, cousins went to beach, so Madam Wong was alone.

The next day she noticed that a window off fire escape of third story apartment was broken. Super was called to fix problem.

That evening she noticed that window was still broken. A inner voice told her not to stay in house until window was fixed.

Second instinct was to call the Super and ask him about problem, and why he left a cigarette in sink. Madam Wong was not able to reach Super, so she shrugged off worry. (Madam Wong later learned that Super had been busy fixing plumbing in neighbors home and had not come to apartment.)

It was a very hot August night, so Madam Wong slept on the couch in living room off fire escape. At four o'clock in the morning, a man quietly crawled through the window, and stepped down on the dining room chair. The chair fell, and Madam Wong saw a silhouette of a man as it hopped from the chair to her. In less than a second, the man straddled her.

Madam Wong saw a clock go off in her head: One thousand one, one thousand two , one thousand three. She knew she had thirty seconds to get man off her, or she would be in trouble.

Man grabbed her wrist and said "Don't say nothin."

She saw man's eyes clearly in moonlight. His pupils were dilated from doing drugs. She could smell liquor on his breath.

Man reached into his pocket to get an object which glistened in moonlight. Madam Wong saw it was a knife. Man planned to rape Madam Wong, to take her pride away, to rob her of most private gifts she save for man she love. Perhaps he kill her, too.

She start to scream loud; so loud she damaged vocal cords. She start to punch man so hard she broke knuckles. She was frightened beyond anything imaginable. Her life so fragile, like tiny gossamer wings of butterfly about to be torn in half.

She heard the rustle of angel wings.

She heard a voice whisper, "He is afraid of getting caught. Keep fighting!"

The man's attention shifted from her, to the front door as he began to look for an escape.

An eternity of seconds later, a burst of light flooded the room as he rushed out the door and down the stairs.

She grabbed her robe and chased him downstairs to the street corner.

She watched him slip into the darkness, never to be seen or heard from again.

Madam Wong went back to the apartment and sat in the dark. Her hands were trembling .

Angel gave her warnings earlier in day.

If she had listened, the man would never have climbed through the window.

"Angels can only do so much," voice tell her, as she stared out into the darkness.

"If you don't listen, how can we help?"

Since that time, Madam Wong always listens for the sound of Angel Wings.

Charity begin at home

I went to college with a most unusual woman. LeLe Chen was very bright and determined, and was what we call a social liberal. She supported a student underground movement in Beijing and later lost her job as school teacher for starting protest over unfair treatment of women. She was up on all the Marxist literature and, if you saw her in narrow setting, you might have thought she was picture of love and equality.

LeLe Chen was anything but. She grew up the baby girl in family of three brothers, and was petted and spoiled by her brothers and parents. She went to the finest boarding school in England, and returned to teach school.

LeLe married a brilliant chemist, and after a few years of marriage, became pregnant. LeLe imagined son would be gifted pianist or scientist, and already began to dream of where to send child to school.

Delivery was very difficult and doctor used forceps. Lele noticed something not so right about boy. She never listened to doctors, and forced child to do more than he could. Boy managed to finish high school before troubles began. Then he began to have hallucinations.

The morning before he was to leave for to college, LeLe found out her son was schizophrenic. Suddenly, the world fell apart for LeLe, as her dreams for son collided with bitter reality.

One year later, son had to be put away in mental hospital.

For years, he would write his mother nearly every day, but she never wrote back. She could not accept that she gave birth to a mentally ill son.

Boy is fifty-five years old now and hasn't seen his mother in 35 years. The staff at hospital have become parents to him. He always asks them if his mother is still alive and why she abandoned him.

If you talk to LeLe, you would never know she had a son, or that she had once been married.

LeLe spends her evenings writing articles on Human Rights.

They tell me, LeLe is famous throughout the world.

Finding little bear

When I was little, Mother gave us stuffed animals to play with. Mother gave me a little white bear with a cute pink nose. This little bear was my very best friend in the world. I dressed her up for tea time, sang lullabies to her, and gave her advice on the ways of the world. Sometime I spanked Little Bear when she was bad and did not do what I wanted. Then she would run to my rocking chair, hide her face and cry. Then I felt sorry I scolded her and told her I spank Little Bear because I love her.

One day, I took little bear to a pond to swim. Little Bear fell into the mud and got dirty. She was no longer a white bear, but a brown bear. When I came home, I hid Little Bear in the drawer with my nightgowns.

Mother discovered Little Bear in the bottom drawer and threw the bear away.

When I found out, I rushed into the streets, searching everywhere for her. Mother say bear no good because she was dirty.

That night, I stared at my plate in silence during dinner, praying for her return.

Something happened, I cannot tell you what. A part of me died with Little Bear. If mother threw out Little

Bear because she fell in the mud, maybe she'll give me away if I make mistake.

I began to see a list of my imperfections, and drew into myself like a plant without water.

It seem there became two me's: The "good" me who sat quietly at dinner. That me didn't fight over biggest pork chop or piece of cake with most icing. That person tip-toed quietly around the house, while the other me wept silently in my rocking chair.

Mother noticed something was wrong.

When she came up to tuck me in, and I looked into her eyes, I realized someone threw her little bear away.

Part of her - the lovely melodious nightingale, was captured and put in a dark cage. I saw in her eyes the suffering and pain of dreams that were buried in unmarked graves. There were no headstones to mark their loss, there was only a silent ache.

A few weeks later, I decided I will find Little Bear in my mind. I will search through all of the trash cans and dumps of Quingdao.

I found Little Bear lying underneath some chicken wings and rice. Together we ran to an enormous waterfall spilling out over a smiling river. I took Little Bear under a magical waterfall and began to scrub her. She began to laugh. She began to dance as the golden rays of sunlight sparkled in the water like precious stones. Little Bear is happy now. Little Bear is home.

*Love and commitment are like two adjoining countries,
you cross the border without realizing it*

Over the years, young women have asked me, "Madam Wong, how did you meet your husband, Wa Shin?"

I was attending college, and wanted to become a concert violinist, but I had to take a Zoology class to get my degree. One day we had to dissect a fetal pig, which was something I could not do. Everyone made fun of me because I could not cut the pig open. Wa Shin volunteered to be my lab partner, and very kindly dissected the pig, while he smiled sheepishly behind his horn rimmed glasses. He was so sweet and bright, I felt very comfortable around him. A lot of the aggressive, "Mr. Athletic" types would ask me out, but I never believed they understood me. I felt like a Stradivarius handled by deaf mutes. Maybe they could pluck my strings, but they could not hear my music.

Wa Shin was painfully shy. So shy, it was hard to tell if he liked me. But something inside me think he hears my music, even though he does not tell me so. I realize pretty soon, I have a crush on him.

Nothing happened for a while. We would speak in the hallway, and he would carry my books, but he didn't appear to be interested. I got so sick of the other boys, I preferred reading alone in my room.

One day, after I had almost given up on Wa Shin, he appeared at my door carrying a single rose.

We went for a long walk along the ocean and talked for hours. I showed him my secret place in the cliffs where I went to day dream and play my violin. Weeks passed, and we laughed and cried and shared secrets with each other. Still I never thought he saw me as anything more than a sister until he shyly gave me a kiss. That evening in the cliffs, we made love together, and I knew he was the person I wanted to grow old with.

Our marriage was a long and beautiful one. We hardly quarreled, and when we did, it is done with respect.

I remember the times he had to take care of me when I was so swollen with our first child I could not even put on my shoes. He gently massaged my feet and helped me dress in the morning. He suffered his own morning sickness during the first few months of our pregnancy, and was patient with me when I was too chubby to roll over in bed without assistance. He helped raise our daughters and was a wonderful father and husband. When his life ended from cancer he died at home, surrounded by those who loved him.

In those last few months of Wa Shin's life, I could finally return all the years of love and devotion he so freely gave me.

It was with honor that I bathed his tiny body that had wasted away so sadly from cancer. It was with honor that I fed him broth, when his hands became so weak that he could not even hold a chopstick. It was with honor that I tucked him in and kissed him good night and said, "Dear one, I love you so," while he gently pressed his hand into mine.

Our love and devotion transcends the five senses. It transcends time itself. I feel his loving presence and know that he is waiting for me. One day we shall be together again in a place very close to the Earth. He says it is beautiful and peaceful there, and I know. It is in my dreams that I meet him there. It is there we share our love.

Even darkest dreams have a silver lining

One Spring afternoon, We Len, a young woman in her thirties, was taking a train to Beijing where she planned to meet her Aunt. A distinguished looking gentleman in his seventies sat down across from her and they began to talk. We Len, an artist, was fascinated to learn that the man was a well known German psychiatrist. Although We Len feel happy, she was plagued by terrible nightmares. We Len tell doctor that she and sister had similar dreams since they were little girls. Doctor asked to hear dream.

"I am on a dirt road. It is hot, and soldiers around me are suffering from heat exhaustion. Men are speaking a language I do not know. I see a man bayoneted by a soldier, and then I see someone decapitated with a machete. A little later, they begin to torture me with something they put in my fingers. Little sticks. I try to hide, but they find me, and then they disembowel me. I wake up in terror and am afraid of the dark."

The doctor ask We Len if her father was a prisoner of war serving in the Pacific.

We Len was very surprised, and said "Yes, he was."

The doctor tell her that he has treated many children of holocaust survivors who had very vivid dreams of gas chambers and starvation, and of the countless acts of dehumanization that occurred from the Nazis. Doctor say that children have these dreams even if parent never talk about their traumatic experiences.

There is a purpose in the dreams.

The sensitive child wishes to heal the parent who is suffering from deep psychic pain. The child's dream is a soulful connection between parent and child. At an unconscious, or spirit level, the child is trying to heal the parent's wounded psyche.

Doctor tell her that the most horrible dreams are the most healing, because the psyche is bringing out repressed memories and allowing them to be acknowledged and processed by the conscious self. He tell her not to fear her nightmares, but to look to them for their meaning.

We Len felt very peaceful about the conversation with the doctor, and very grateful.

It reminded her of the times she would see her father sitting alone in the darkness with a glass of wine.

She remembers hopping in his lap and putting her hand on his face. Tears were on her fingertips.

Her heart opened up like a large ocean, wanting to wash over all his pain.

He trembled like a wounded animal who had staggered off quietly into the forest night.

He mumbled softly that maybe it would have been better if he had died with his comrades.

"We love you Daddy," she said to him as he squeezed her hand softly as tears rolled gently down his cheeks.

We Len say she never had nightmares again.

Blame is like quicksand...easy to get into, difficult to get out of

One thing Madam Wong really hate, is to be asked to referee a fight between husband and wife. There is no sadder sight than to watch a couple hop into ring like two roosters at a cock fight. To slash each other with their claws and beaks, until one is lying face down in a pool of blood, while the other crows atop a self righteous dung heap.

What lead couples to such unhappiness and destruction?

When couples marry, they are optimistic and idealize one another.

Each partner is more likely to examine his or her own faults, and give mate benefit of doubt.

As time pass, the husband and wife's shortcomings begin to surface.

Many people are deeply wounded when they discover their partner isn't perfect.

Egos take center stage, and winning becomes more important than solving problem.

When couples begin to blame each other, they move into marital quicksand, where they are stuck in opposing views. Sinking deeper and deeper, they disappear under a murky bog of resentments and blame.

What can you do to turn around a marriage which is going under by blame and mean talk?

Madam Wong say it will take one partner who is committed to love, patience, and forgiveness. That partner must stand firm in love and peace, when the other spouse puts on his boxing gloves.

Instead of playing the guilt or blame game, the loving partner could fix her mate's favorite meal, or suggest that he enjoy swimming at health club, while she takes care of children. Such selfless acts might leave the partner's mouth gaping open in surprise and respect.

Madam Wong can't help but think of John F. Kennedy's speech, and modify it to:

> "Ask not what your beloved can do for you,
> Ask what you can do for your beloved."

You may snicker at such old-fashioned idealism, but it works.

As new pattern continue, the other spouse may begin to respond in a loving manner. (How long can one partner shadow box to his own image before it gets boring?) Remember relationship is about two people, and if you want to change a relationship, you must first change yourself.

When storm of emotion pass, seek shelter

I never met a woman whose emotions didn't ebb and flow like the ocean tide.

Most of the time, feelings come and go in rhythms of purpose and consistency. Like ocean, our emotional tides wax and wane with the seasons of the year, and the seasons of our life. Sometime, a storm of emotion approaches with such force that we feel like we are drowning. If we struggle and resist feelings, it only make matters worse.

Sometimes, a situational storm develops. Other times, it may be "flooding" waves of fear, or grief rising up from the unconscious.

As emotional typhoon approach, imagine yourself safely strapped to the rails of a boat. As waves begin to sweep over you, breathe deeply, and tell yourself it will pass. Call a friend. Don't be afraid to ask for help.

And never forget that feelings, even the nutty ones, are part of you and deserve respect. Say to self ,"Yes, I'm crazy now, but I've been crazy before, and got over it."

That help me, when I would say to poor Wa Shin, "Strap me to a gurney and take me to Bellevue." He knew to give me wide birth.

But just when I thought I couldn't take one more gallon of salt water, the sunlight and the seagull's announced I was in safe harbor.

Are you a light on someone's path (or a hidden ditch)

Sometimes, while moving through life, I felt alone. As I carried a lantern up a steep cliff in the darkness, strangers cloaked in confusion silently passed by. They wearily descended the path with eyes glazed over in grief.

It seem as though I was invisible to the whole human race.

But I was wrong, for even in life's darkest hour, I have never been alone.

The mysterious universe, in all its grace, has always provided a light-bearer in front of my path.

Sometimes, there have been kind strangers who showed the way around a single turn, and whose name I cannot recall. Others have lifted me up to a safe spot in the cliff, when I didn't have the strength to pull myself up. Some have silently shared their supper, and when I looked up to thank them, they were gone.

A few, like my dearest mother, have been a beacon in the night, giving solace to the weary traveler.

Think of the thousands of faces who have greeted you since you came into this world. Of all the hands that have caressed you and nurtured you since you were a baby.

All the family, friends, teachers, and Good Samaritans who have silently shared their light and love with you.

How can you ever feel alone when so many people have touched you?

And as you look in the mirror and frown at those age lines, think of all the acts of kindness you have quietly done for others; sincere, heartfelt acts of generosity you have bestowed on another life traveler. How can you possibly ever know how many lives you have touched?

Kindness is a link between each and every soul.

If you are feeling sad and alone, imagine all those caring people standing in front of you. Imagine all the people you have helped along the way and let them sit at your fireside.

How can you be alone when the room is filled with hundreds of spirits whose lives you have touched?

In the sixties, my children left home
And had families of their own.
It was only Wa Shin and me.
(How do you cook for two?)
My heart was so heavy
I sought refuge in books.
Hundreds of them.
I became obsessed with Western philosophy
and literature.
I even wrote poetry.

Here are a few of them...

The farmer

In the stillness of a cold March morning, the farmer plants his first seeds for summer.

With a spade, he gently furrows out a long tube, so that the seed may be planted deep.

He inspects the seeds carefully, to plant those which show the most promise. Sometimes, he may plant an odd shaped, sickly seed, just to test his judgment. Secretly, he hopes that the seed with the seeming of the least potential might produce the best fruit. That would make his heart sing and would bring him great luck. The heavens smile upon such things, the farmer thought, and grace the man who believes in the unseen, and who understands that beyond all vulnerability, is great strength. Didn't the oak start as a tiny seed which could not be easily distinguished from the others?

The farmer pats down the final clump of earth and silently wipes a tear from his eye.

He has done all he can, and there is some sadness in that. He will attend to the unborn plants by providing water, if nature does not, and by keeping the wild animals away. But he cannot guarantee that his efforts will produce trees that his grandchildren can climb in, or fruit that his family can eat. But he is a wise man and learned years ago that all things have their own time to grow, and that it is different for each one.

He understands, that in his impatience and fear, he cannot unearth the seed to see if it has sprouted. He cannot sit cross-legged in front of garden while the sun rises and sets, willing the plants to grow. Only a mad man does such things, yet the world is filled with mad men who never learned that less is more. They never learned to plant the seed, send out a prayer and release it to its own fate.

The farmer has had good years of great abundance and lean years of lack.

Through it all, he plants his seeds like he is planting them today, in the stillness of a cold March morning, and sends his love into each and every tiny bulb. For he is a farmer, and a man of faith.

Manhattan yaks

Like their Himalayan cousins who inhabit
The high plateaus of Tibet,
Manhattan Yaks are a rarefied breed
Living in a rarefied world:
The exalted heights of glass and steel
Where the air is thin.

Like their plodding, four-hoofed brethren,
Manhattan Yaks are beasts of burden
    - the corporate variety -
Who have traded in their yoke and plow
For a CBS tote bag and sky pager.

The geometrically coiffured clones
Are goaded into labor
Not by the whip, but by the corporate totem
Whom they kneel in prayer for, a la mantra,
And kill the fattened calf.

The graven image replaces God, family, morality.
The nihilistic taskmaster has even replaced sex.
For in the swirling waters of the Vertical Club
And at parties in the Hamptons,

Yaks chatter narcoleptically
About their Orwellian God.

The white-collar "Step-in-fetchits"
Live in a Walter Mitty World.
For in their pea-sized craniums
They begin to superimpose their image
Over the corporate logo.
They begin to believe it is THEY who control the taskmaster.

About that time the beasts are sent to slaughter.
Their erudite heads roll off the chopping block
Splattering onto the pavement far below.
Unnoticed, the bloody mass is trampled by the herd
Plodding to and fro in the noisy street.

The invisible ones

In the ghetto they reside
In the rat-infested hovels
Of darkness and despair.
Theirs is a sad lot
Of broken dreams and needle tracks, poverty and death.
Kindness, as scarce of a commodity as food.

Behind the boarded-up windows of abandoned buildings
The young are taught the language of the street.
Prostitution, thievery and murder are the order of the
day.
The price of flesh is cheap;
The women sell their bodies for an evenings fix.

The sweltering heat of an August night
Brings the children out to play in open fire-hydrants
While the parents slouch against a stoop,
Roll a reefer, crack a joke, snort some coke.
The cries of infants muffled
By the roar of a rumbling subway.

Graffiti is their art work.
Bars and X-rated movies,
The entertainment of the hour.

Young men strut like cocks of the walk.
Kings of the shit pile,
They mask their tears with anger and bravado.

Faces frozen in a shark-like stare
Their usefulness and self-respect are bottled up and
thrown out to sea
Before they reach the age of ten.
The girls, juicy and ripe at fourteen,
Wither on the vine by twenty-five.

Society's lepers; the invisible ones are left to rot
in their own hopelessness
With nothing but a dime-bag and a stiletto in their
pockets,
They quietly board a train bound for nowhere.

Summer song
(For Wa Shin)

There's a trembling in my heart.
As I look within the garden of our memories,
That blossom forth like tiny rose buds in the spring.
Warm and inviting, the remembrance is sweet
Like Summer's gentle kiss.

Beneath the lover's sighs
You held my dreams in your hands,
And gazed upon my soul unbound.
Ferried to a distant isle where dreams are made
I felt safe, dear one,
Like a child's forgotten lullaby
Whispered softly in the night.
Unmasked joy, I felt,
Standing proudly before your humanity
Unfolding, like a gentle summer flower.

The Cherry tree

One day, amid a magnificent forest of pine trees, a tiny cherry blossom seed blew in with the March wind.

It settled itself alongside a group of young pines and happily took root.

Within a few years, the Cherry tree grew large enough to see its own reflection in a pond which lay a small distance away. The tree realized for the first time that it was different from the others. Its limbs were longer, and its leaves were flat. It longed to look just like the other trees, whose branches were filled with dark green needles and decorative pine cones.

That night, the Cherry tree prayed silently to itself. It wished to be as lovely as the other trees.

Within a few weeks, something miraculous happened. Beautiful pink blossoms began to flower on the tree. The pine trees talked among themselves about this strange sight, admiring for the first time the Cherry tree's unique beauty. The tree's spirit danced in delight at the magnificence of its own reflection. A group of children with their parents came by to admire the tree, and take its picture. Life was truly grand, the Cherry tree thought. Finally it would get the love and admiration that it had longed for. But the tree's glory was short-lived. Within a few weeks, the blossoms lay strewn on the moist spring grass.

The Cherry tree wondered what all the glory had been about, and was disappointed that the lovely blossoms were so short-lived. Still, it was summer, and the warm sunlight made the pond shimmer like diamonds. A family of Robins made their nest in one of the Cherry tree's branches, and a woman with golden hair spent long, intoxicating afternoons underneath the Cherry tree's bough, reading poetry. The tree felt so alive and part of nature. Days melted dreamily into one another like liquid gold, until finally, the summer passed. Weeks went by and the Cherry tree wondered where the children were. He was told by the older Pines that they had gone off to school. A few weeks later, the earth began to cool and the Cherry tree noticed that its leaves were changing colour again. This time they turned golden, and later a brilliant red. The Cherry tree loved the fall colours almost as much as the spring blossoms, and felt a new found euphoria and wisdom. The Pines seemed to be much less affected by the seasons as they looked and felt the same year round. The Cherry tree was sad it did not have anyone to share its joys or sorrows with.

As fall turned into winter, the wind whipped unmercifully through the valley.

One November night, a very strong rain storm pelted the forest with little frozen balls of ice. The next morning, the Cherry tree awoke and shrieked in horror when it saw its own reflection in the pond. Now the tree began to cry out in pain at its own nakedness. None of the Pines had ever seen a tree lose its leaves during the winter, and made fun of the Cherry tree. They talked among themselves about how damned ugly the tree was, saying they wished a woodcutter would chop it down. They said the Cherry tree was an eyesore and a freak of nature that made the rest of the Pines look bad. The Cherry tree bent its head in shame at its own nakedness, and did not speak a word. Shivering in shame and despair, the tree pondered its fate. It wondered why it had to suffer so when the other trees seemed to be indifferent to the winters. What had it done to deserve the cruelty of nature, and even worse, the hateful rejection from the "normal" pines? All seemed lost.

Winter slowly passed until one spring morning, a large Fir cried out that he saw tiny green buds on the Cherry tree. A few weeks later, the fragrant pink blossoms returned, and the summer passed as magically as the year before. Then came the fall, and the cycle repeated itself.

Each year the Cherry tree seemed to die and be reborn, while the other Pine trees remained the same.

One December day, as the snow fell gently on the frozen pond, a young woman came to visit to the Cherry tree. She was one of the tree's admirers who had taken its picture in spring, when it's blossoms were in full bloom. The tree recognized her as the young woman with dancing blue eyes and golden hair, and asked her why she had come to visit in the winter when he was ugly and alone. He had nothing to offer but his sadness. She smiled at the tree and gently took off her scarf. The Cherry tree expected to see her long golden hair, but saw instead, a bald head without a single strand of hair.

"I have lost my leaves too," she told the tree. "Once I had beautiful flowing hair, but I am sick, and the treatment the doctors gave me made my hair fall out". The tree began to weep in understanding of her loss.

The woman told the tree that one day, her hair would grow back again. She vowed to let it grow wild and free, like a horse's mane. But the woman said the illness was a strange kind of gift that gave new meaning to her life. "Constancy is not a measure of happiness.

Some of the happiest people are those who experience life passionately; both the pleasure and the pain. They drink in all of life's joys and sorrows. For without sorrow, how would you know real joy?

There is a beauty and purpose in suffering, and it gives dignity to the human condition."

The Cherry tree had never looked at life that way.

Certainly he recalled his anticipation of spring was greater than the other trees, and seemed to enjoy and appreciate the Summers even more.

Yes, looking at the young woman's face, he realized that suffering had transformed her. She was more vulnerable, more alive. And he saw in her eyes, a tenderness and understanding that was even more beautiful than the carefree face with the long golden hair that had danced beneath his bough during the balmy days of summer. Here, underneath the cold, frozen, gray sky, amid the slumbering earth, the Cherry tree saw a face alive with the spirit of life. The will to live, despite pain and suffering. Yes, that is beauty, the Cherry tree thought, as he lost himself in her radiance, which filled the heavens like a choir of golden angels.

The Cherry tree looked out at the frozen earth and saw that it was brimming over with life. He saw the tracks in the snow of a cottontail rabbit, who was out foraging food for its family. A pair of barn owls huddled nearby in an old tin shed where a farmer stored wood for Winter. Fish lay in suspended animation below the frozen lake, their hearts beating slower, yet beating just the same. Over the hill, smoke rose above a chimney, where below it, a plump, happy farmer's wife made breakfast for her brood.

The young woman reached in her bag, and pulled out some Christmas tree ornaments. She began to wrap the Cherry tree with green and gold ribbons. The Cherry tree began to laugh a deep, thunderous laugh until its limbs began to shake so that it awoke a sleeping brown bird from its winter nap.

Now both the tree and the young woman laughed until they cried at the sheer beauty of existence.

The young woman reached out and put her arms around the Cherry tree's trunk while the two said a silent prayer. "Let us promise to live life to the fullest... each and every day. Let us laugh at our own vanity, and even at our own misery sometimes. Let us rejoice in the magical, mysterious and wondrous gift of life, for all its joys and sorrows. For it is good."

Endings and beginnings

When I think of the hundreds of young girls who have sat at my table and poured out their gentle, trembling hearts to me, my eyes become misty and my heart overflows with gratitude at the privilege of bearing witness to their unfolding.

What exquisite joy to see their faces change, from doe-eyed girl, to proud young women with children of their own. To see wrinkles lining the corners of their eyes, as testimony to life's passages...

For all the crushes and hurt feelings and joys and disappointments. For the girls who became famous and for those who did not. Those who married and those who stayed single. Each event I remember as though it were yesterday.

Was I ever a young girl? Am I really an old woman?

I remember each event as equal distance from me.

Watching my mother comb her hair before the mirror, and wishing I would become as beautiful as her. Longing for firm round breasts. Longing to experience my first kiss. Longing to make a difference in the world. Longing to have a husband and children of my own. Longing to be needed and loved. Longing to age with grace. Longing to have purpose and to be forever young at heart.

Who does not remember these dreams?

I often see my dear mother as she was when she was thirty. She is ninety-three now, but I still remember that beautiful young woman putting on perfume and grooming herself as she waited for my father to come home. I remember her tucking me in at night.

The smell of her perfume and her angelic eyes. So courageous, so gracious, so wise.

Time cannot fade that memory, for there are really no beginnings or endings.

Love is what ties the present, past, and future together.

Love even keeps us in contact with departed souls who have given up their bodies for a different world.

It is of great comfort, as it reminds me that there are really no endings, there is only change.

Know that all the people who have ever loved you, still love you. They are a candle burning brightly in your heart.

I am here in spirit as you read my words, and am sending love and best wishes to you.

Love cannot be contained by time or space.

Rejoice in that love, for it is yours.

Eliza Bussey grew up in Oklahoma, in a colorful household. Her mother, Mary Ruth, is a "Southern Aunte Mame." In 1941, this 15-year-old anthropology enthusiast and aviator, became the country's youngest female pilot.

Eliza's father, Hez Bussey, was a survivor of the infamous Bataan Death March, and was a Prisoner of War by the Japanese during World War Two.

This part-Cherokee Indian, part-Irish Judge of the Court of Criminal Appeals, could recite Kipling with a style that rivaled the best of Britain.

Eliza's sister Susan, a lawyer, and travel hound, has been a Tribal Judge for the Ute Indians, and lawyer for the Federated States of Micronesia. She is also fond of Bassets.

In high school, Eliza studied Drama and Martial Arts. At 21, she was rated second in the world, in Full Contact Karate, appeared on "Wide World of Sports," and was the first woman to ever fight a man in Madison Square Garden. Living in New York City after graduating from the University of Oklahoma with a degree in Journalism, she taught martial arts and worked as a stage hand at the Metropolitan Opera House.

Before embarking on a career as a writer, Eliza worked as a television reporter in El Paso Texas, covering Mexican Mafia trials and rattlesnake roundups. She now resides in Washington, D.C. where she works as a television producer and trains in Wu Shu.